THE POETRY OF CATS

Dobra Koczka ktera nemlsa

Das ist eine gute Katz die nicht Nascht

A good cat *Wenceslaus Hollar*

The Poetry of Cats

edited by Samuel Carr

LONGMEADOW
P R E S S

This 1991 edition published by
Longmeadow Press
201 High Ridge Road
Stamford CT 06904

in association with Reed International Books Limited

ISBN 0-681-41182-1

First published in Great Britain in 1974 by
B. T. Batsford Limited
Second edition, with additions 1980

Produced by Mandarin Offset
Printed in Hong Kong

0 9 8 7 6 5 4 3 2

Contents

Acknowledgements

The Publishers would like to thank the following for permission to
include certain copyright poems:
Patrick Chalmers, *The Tortoiseshell Cat* (from A PECK O'MAUT): Methuen
& Co. Ltd.
Richard Church, *The Cat* (from COLLECTED POEMS, William Heinemann
Ltd): The Estate of the late Richard Church.
Elizabeth Coatsworth, *Calling in the Cat*. Reprinted by permission of
Coward, McCann and Geoghegan, Inc., from COMPASS ROSE by
Elizabeth Coatsworth. Copyright 1929, renewed © 1957, by Elizabeth
Coatsworth.
W. H. Davies, *The Cat*. Copyright © 1963 by Jonathan Cape Ltd.
Reprinted from THE POEMS OF W. H. DAVIES by permission of Mrs H. M.
Davies, Jonathan Cape Ltd, London and the Wesleyan University
Press, Connecticut.
T. S. Eliot, *The Song of the Jellicles* (from OLD POSSUM'S BOOK OF
PRACTICAL CATS by T. S. Eliot, copyright 1939, by T. S. Eliot, copyright,
1967, by Esme Valerie Eliot). Reprinted by permission of Faber and
Faber Ltd, London, and Harcourt Brace Jovanovich Inc., New York.
Annabel Farjeon, *Ode to a Fat Cat*: Mrs I. Anrep.

The Illustrations

Introduction

Compared to the number of poems about birds or flowers,
or for that matter about dogs, there are relatively few about
cats. The reason is obvious. A cat, like a beautiful landscape,
exists self-sufficiently and in its own right. Just as painters
have seldom found it possible to make a notable "view" the
subject for their art—what nature has satisfactorily achieved
inhibits representation or transliteration: how many good
pictures are there of the Alps?—so the perfection and
detachment of the Cat have deterred all but a small number
of poets from writing on the theme. Birds and flowers can
both provide the basis for a poetic moral or a human parallel.
Not so the Cat, whose independence resists sentimentality
and anthropomorphism alike. (Not but what the Cat has not
on occasion been the pretext for a moral, whether fabulously
by La Fontaine, domestically by Cowper, or in the most
famous of all Cat poems, by Gray).

For the painter, who is under no compulsion to draw
morals, the Cat's remoteness and perfection have indeed
often proved attractive. There may not be many cat portraits,
apart from one or two marvellously feline paintings by
Bonnard in which the high-arched backs of the subjects
dictate a narrow upright canvas; and the pair of disreputable
roof-top cats which Manet so vividly depicts. The rule in
general is that the cat is incidental to the picture's ostensible
subject, as in Hogarth's *Graham Children* where, enlarged, the
cat that strains after the bird in the cage could as well be a
tiger. One thinks too of the cats that have been painted or
drawn by Delacroix, Renoir, Rembrandt, Gainsborough,
Steinlen and Aubrey Beardsley (but not, a little surprisingly,
by Carpaccio). Or of the cats of fantasy of Edward Lear,
Louis Wain, Grandville and Beatrix Potter (though with
Beatrix Potter fantasy and reality are inextricably connected;
for all that they are dressed in Edwardian clothes no cats

could be more feline than Ribby, Tom Kitten, and Mrs Tabitha Twitchit).

It would be easy to make a list of the major writers in whose works no cats appear. There is scarcely a cat to be found in the length and breadth of *The Bible*. Shylock charitably mentions the "harmless necessary cat", but Shakespeare's other references are slighting and few. A similar indifference to the cat is shown in the works of Milton and Donne, Dryden and Pope, Blake (unexpectedly) and Burns, Byron and Shelley. Across the Channel, in France at least, a poetic climate more favourable to the cat is reflected in verse by Jules Lemaitre, François Coppée, Paul Verlaine, Hippolyte Taine and Pierre Béranger, while the two or three cat poems of Charles Baudelaire are perhaps the finest that have been written in any language. Like all poetry, they are un-translatable, so one has here been reproduced in the original French.

Most inexplicable is the absence of American cat poems. Fifty years ago Carl Van Vechten remarked on a deficiency which has hardly been made up in the interval. T. S. Eliot, if he may be allowed to be American, has to some extent repaired the omission, and there have been contributions of a different kind from Don Marquis and Elizabeth Coatsworth. But from Whitman and Longfellow, Poe and Emerson, Melville and Lowell, or from twentieth-century writers such as Robert Frost, e. e. cummings and Theodore Roethke, only silence and apparent indifference. The tailpiece in this collection, by J. G. Whittier, does little enough either in its length or quality to right the balance. What can be the explanation of such neglect on the part of a nation that is fond of animals and fruitful in poets?

The prose of cats is another story and a longer one. It proved impossible to resist the temptation to represent this story, at least by the inclusion of Dr Johnson's Hodge and Montaigne's anonymous playfellow.

As to the pictures, they do not attempt to *illustrate* the poems: heaven forbid. They may, however, act as a visual counterpart to the verse, abstracting by their details something of the same feline essence as the poets convey in words.

C

C was Papa's gray Cat,
   Who caught a squeaky Mouse;
She pulled him by his twirly tail
   All about the house.

EDWARD LEAR

C was Papa's gray Cat *Edward Lear*

The Song of the Jellicles

Jellicle Cats come out to-night
Jellicle Cats come one come all:
The Jellicle Moon is shining bright—
Jellicles come to the Jellicle Ball.

Jellicle Cats are black and white,
Jellicle Cats are rather small;
Jellicle Cats are merry and bright,
And pleasant to hear when they caterwaul.
Jellicle Cats have cheerful faces,
Jellicle Cats have bright black eyes;
They like to practise their airs and graces
And wait for the Jellicle Moon to rise.

Jellicle Cats develop slowly,
Jellicle Cats are not too big;
Jellicle Cats are roly-poly,
They know how to dance a gavotte and a jig.
Until the Jellicle Moon appears
They make their toilette and take their repose:
Jellicles wash behind their ears,
Jellicles dry between their toes.

Jellicle Cats are white and black,
Jellicle Cats are of moderate size;
Jellicles jump like a jumping-jack,
Jellicle Cats have moonlit eyes.

They're quiet enough in the morning hours,
They're quiet enough in the afternoon,
Reserving their terpsichorean powers
To dance by the light of the Jellicle Moon.

Jellicle Cats are black and white,
Jellicle Cats (as I said) are small;
If it happens to be a stormy night
They will practise a caper or two in the hall.
If it happens the sun is shining bright
You would say they had nothing to do at all:
They are resting and saving themselves to be right
For the Jellicle Moon and the Jellicle Ball.

T. S. ELIOT

Detail of an illustration by Randolph Caldecott

Calling in the cat

Now from the dark, a deeper dark,
The cat slides,
Furtive and aware,
His eyes still shine with meteor spark
The cold dew weights his hair.
Suspicious,
Hesitant, he comes
Stepping morosely from the night,
Held but repelled,
Repelled but held,
By lamp and firelight.

Now call your blandest,
Offer up
The sacrifice of meat,
And snare the wandering soul with greeds,
Give him to drink and eat,
And he shall walk fastidiously
Into the trap of old
On feet that still smell delicately
Of withered ferns and mould.

ELIZABETH COATSWORTH

From a woodcut by Thomas Bewick

The death of a cat

For he was our puck, our miniature lar, he fluttered
Our dovecot of visiting cards, he flicked them askew.
The joker among them who made a full house. As you said,
He was a fine cat. Though how strange to have, as you said later,
Such a personal sense of loss. And looking aside
You said, but unconvincingly: What does it matter?

★   ★   ★   ★

To begin with he was a beautiful object:
Blue crisp fur with a white collar,
Paws of white velvet, springs of steel,
A Pharaoh's profile, a Krishna's grace,
Tail like a questionmark at a masthead
And eyes dug out of a mine, not the dark
Clouded tarns of a dog's, but cat's eyes—
Light in a rock crystal, light distilled
Before his time and ours, before cats were tame.

To continue, he was alive and young,
A dancer, incurably male, a clown,
With his gags, his mudras, his entrechats,
His triple bends and his double takes,
Firm as a Rameses in African wonderstone,
Fluid as Krishna chasing the milkmaids,
Who hid under carpets and nibbled at olives,
Attacker of ankles, nonesuch of nonsense,
Indolent, impudent, cat catalytic.

To continue further: if not a person
More than a cipher, if not affectionate
More than indifferent, if not volitive
More than automaton, if not self-conscious
More than mere conscious, if not useful
More than a parasite, if allegorical

More than heraldic, if man-conditioned
More than a gadget, if perhaps a symbol
More than a symbol, if somewhat a proxy
More than a stand-in—was what he was!
A self-contained life, was what he must be
And is not now: more than an object.

And is not now. Spreadeagled on coverlets—
Those are the coverlets, bouncing on chairbacks—
These are the chairs, pirouetting and sidestepping,
Feinting and jabbing, breaking a picture frame—
Here is the picture, tartar and sybarite,
One minute quicksilver, next minute butterballs,
Precise as a fencer, lax as an odalisque,
And in his eyes the light from the mines
One minute flickering, steady the next,
Lulled to a glow or blown to a blaze,
But always the light that was locked in the stone
Before his time and ours; at best semi-precious
All stones of that kind yet, if not precious,
Are more than stones, beautiful objects
But more than objects. While there is light in them.

LOUIS MACNEICE

Esther's Tomcat

Daylong this tomcat lies stretched flat
As an old rough mat, no mouth and no eyes.
Continual wars and wives are what
Have tattered his ears and battered his head.

Like a bundle of old rope and iron
Sleeps till blue dusk. Then reappear
His eyes, green as ringstones: he yawns wide red,
Fangs fine as a lady's needle and bright.

A tomcat sprang at a mounted knight,
Locked round his neck like a trap of hooks
While the knight rode fighting its clawing and bite.
After hundreds of years the stain's there

On the stone where he fell, dead of the tom:
That was at Barnborough. The tomcat still
Grallochs odd dogs on the quiet,
Will take the head clean off your simple pullet,

Is unkillable. From the dog's fury,
From gunshot fired point-blank he brings
His skin whole, and whole
From owlish moons of bekittenings

Among ashcans. He leaps and lightly
Walks upon sleep, his mind on the moon.
Nightly over the round world of men,
Over the roofs go his eyes and outcry.

TED HUGHES

From a woodcut by Thomas Bewick

Detail of an illustration by Randolph Caldecott

Five eyes

In Hans' old mill his three black cats
Watch the bins for the thieving rats.
Whisker and claw, they crouch in the night,
Their five eyes smouldering green and bright:
Squeaks from the flour sacks, squeaks from where
The cold wind stirs on the empty stair,
Squeaking and scampering everywhere.
Then down they pounce, now in, now out,
At whisking tail, and sniffing snout;
While lean old Hans, he snores away
Till peep of light and break of day;
Then up he climbs to his creaking mill,
Out come his cats all grey with meal,
Jekkel, and Jessop and one-eyed Jill.

WALTER DE LA MARE

Cats

Cats sleep
Anywhere,
Any table,
Any chair,
Top of piano,
Window-ledge,
In the middle,
On the edge,
Open drawer,
Empty shoe,
Anybody's
Lap will do,
Fitted in a
Cardboard box,
In the cupboard
With your frocks—
Anywhere!
They don't care!
Cats sleep
Anywhere.

ELEANOR FARJEON

From a drawing by G. B. Tiepolo

25

Milk for the cat

When the tea is brought at five o'clock,
And all the neat curtains are drawn with care,
The little black cat with bright green eyes
Is suddenly purring there.

At first she pretends, having nothing to do,
She has come in merely to blink by the grate,
But, though tea may be late and the milk may be sour,
She is never late.

And presently her agate eyes
Take a soft large milky haze,
And her independent casual glance
Becomes a stiff hard gaze.

Then she stamps her claws or lifts her ears
Or twists her tail and begins to stir,
Till suddenly all her lithe body becomes
One breathing trembling purr.

The children eat and wriggle and laugh;
The two old ladies stroke their silk:
But the cat is grown small and thin with desire,
Transformed to a creeping lust for milk.

The white saucer like some full moon descends
At last from the clouds of the table above;
She sighs and dreams and thrills and glows,
Transfigured with love.

She nestles over the shining rim,
Buries her chin in the creamy sea;
Her tail hangs loose; each drowsy paw
Is doubled under each bending knee.

A long dim ecstasy holds her life;
Her world is an infinite shapeless white,
Till her tongue has curled the last holy drop,
Then she sinks back into the night.

Draws and dips her body to heap
Her sleepy nerves in the great arm-chair,
Lies defeated and buried deep
Three or four hours unconscious there.

HAROLD MONRO

Detail of an illustration to Hudibras.
From an engraving by William Hogarth

Last words to a dumb friend

Pet was never mourned as you,
Purrer of the spotless hue,
Plumy tail, and wistful gaze,
While you humoured our queer ways,
Or outshrilled your morning call
Up the stairs and through the hall—
Foot suspended in its fall—
While, expectant, you would stand
Arched, to meet the stroking hand;
Till your way you chose to wend
Yonder, to your tragic end.

Never another pet for me!
Let your place all vacant be;
Better blankness day by day
Than companion torn away.
Better bid his memory fade,
Better blot each mark he made,
Selfishly escape distress
By contrived forgetfulness,
Than preserve his prints to make
Every morn and eve an ache.

From the chair whereon he sat
Sweep his fur, nor wince thereat;
Rake his little pathways out
Mid the bushes roundabout;
Smooth away his talons' mark
From the claw-worn pine-tree bark,
Where he climbed as dusk enbrowned
Waiting us who loitered round.

Strange it is this speechless thing,
Subject to our mastering,

Subject for his life and food
To our gift, and time, and mood;
Timid pensioner of us Powers,
His existence ruled by ours,
Should—by crossing at a breath
Into safe and shielded death,
By the merely taking hence
Of his insignificance—
Loom as largened to the sense,
Shape as part, above man's will,
Of the Imperturbable.

As a prisoner, flight debarred,
Exercising in a yard,
Still retain I, troubled, shaken,
Mean estate, by him forsaken;
And this home, which scarcely took
Impress from his little look,
By his faring to the Dim,
Grows all eloquent of him.

Housemate, I can think you still
Bounding to the window-sill,
Over which I vaguely see
Your small mound beneath the tree,
Showing in the autumn shade
That you moulder where you played.

THOMAS HARDY

Le rendez-vous des chats *Edouard Manet*

The cat and the moon

The cat went here and there
And the moon spun round like a top
And the nearest kin of the moon,
The creeping cat, looked up.
Black Minnaloushe stared at the moon,
For, wander and wail as he would,
The pure cold light in the sky
Troubled his animal blood.
Minnaloushe runs in the grass
Lifting his delicate feet.
Do you dance, Minnaloushe, do you dance?
When two close kindred meet,
What better than call a dance?
Maybe the moon may learn,
Tired of that courtly fashion
A new dance turn.
Minnaloushe creeps through the grass
From moonlit place to place,
The sacred moon overhead
Has taken a new phase.
Does Minnaloushe know that his pupils
Will pass from change to change,
And that from round to crescent,
From crescent to round they range?
Minnaloushe creeps through the grass
Alone, important and wise,
And lifts to the changing moon
His changing eyes.

W. B. YEATS

Cat

Dear creature by the fire a-purr,
  Strange idol, eminently bland,
Miraculous puss! As o'er your fur
  I trail a negligible hand,

And gaze into your gazing eyes,
  And wonder in a demi-dream,
What mystery it is that lies,
  Behind those slits that glare and gleam,

An exquisite enchantment falls
  About the portals of my sense;
Meandering through enormous halls,
  I breathe luxurious frankincense,

An ampler air, a warmer June
  Enfold me, and my wondering eye
Salutes a more imperial moon
  Throned in a more resplendent story

Than ever knew this northern shore.
  Oh, strange! For you are with me too,
And I who am a cat once more
  Follow the woman that was you

With tail erect and pompous march,
  The proudest puss that ever trod,
Through many a grove, 'neath many an arch,
  Impenetrable as a god.

Down many an alabaster flight
  Of broad and cedar-shaded stairs,
While over us the elaborate night
  Mysteriously gleams and glares.

LYTTON STRACHEY

from:

The kitten and falling leaves

See the kitten on the wall
Sporting with the leaves that fall,
Withered leaves-one-two-and three—
From the lofty elder tree!

    ★   ★   ★   ★

—But the kitten, how she starts,
Crouches, stretches, paws, and darts!
First at one, and then its fellow
Just as light and just as yellow;
There are many now—now one—
Now they stop and there are none.
What intenseness of desire
In her upward eye of fire!
With a tiger-leap half way
Now she meets the coming prey,
Lets it go as fast, and then
Has it in her power again:
Now she works with three or four,
Like an Indian conjurer,
Quick as he in feats of art,
Far beyond in joy of heart. . . .

WILLIAM WORDSWORTH

The cat

Hark! She is calling to her cat.
She is down the misty garden in a tatter-brim straw hat,
And broken slippers grass-wet, treading tearful daisies.
But he does not heed her. He sits still—and gazes.

Where the laden gooseberry leans over to the rose,
He sits, thorn-protected, gazing down his nose.
Coffee-coloured skies above him press upon the sun;
Bats about his mistress flitter-flutter one by one;

Jessamines drop perfume; the nightingales begin;
Nightjars wind their humdrum notes; a crescent moon rides
    thin;
The daybird chorus dies away, the air shrinks chill and grey.
Her lonely voice still calls him—but her panther won't
    come in!

RICHARD CHURCH

34

Chat sur une balustrade *Théophile Steinlen*

Diamond cut diamond

Two cats
One up a tree
One under the tree
The cat up a tree is he
The cat under the tree is she
The tree is witch elm, just incidentally.
He takes no notice of she, she takes no notice of he.
He stares at the woolly clouds passing, she stares at the tree.
There's been a lot written about cats, by Old Possum, Yeats and
Company
But not Alfred de Musset or Lord Tennyson or Poe or anybody
Wrote about one cat under, and one cat up, a tree.
God knows why this should be left for me
Except I like cats as cats be
Especially one cat up
And one cat under
A witch elm
Tree.

EWART MILNE

The cat of the house

Over the hearth with my 'minishing eyes I muse
Until after
The last coal dies.
Every tunnel of the mouse,
Every channel of the cricket,
I have smelt.
I have felt
The secret shifting of the mouldered rafter,
And heard
Every bird in the thicket.
I see
You
Nightingale up in your tree!
I, born of a race of strange things,
Of deserts, great temples, great kings,
In the hot sands where the nightingale never sings!

FORD MADOX FORD

From a woodcut by Thomas Bewick

The cat

Within that porch, across the way,
   I see two naked eyes this night;
Two eyes that neither shut nor blink,
   Searching my face with a green light.

But cats to me are strange, so strange
   I cannot sleep if one is near;
And though I'm sure I see those eyes,
   I'm not so sure a body's there!

W. H. DAVIES

From a Regency-period woodcut

My old cat

My old cat is dead,
Who would butt me with his head.
He had the sleekest fur.
He had the blackest purr.
Always gentle with us
Was this black puss,
But when I found him to-day
Stiff and cold where he lay
His look was a lion's,
Full of rage, defiance:
Oh, he would not pretend
That what came was a friend
But met it in pure hate.
Well died, my old cat.

HAL SUMMERS

Cats

Cats, no less liquid than their shadows,
Offer no angles to the wind,
They slip, diminished, neat, through loopholes
Less than themselves; will not be pinned

To rules or routes for journeys; counter
Attack with non-resistance; twist
Enticing through the curving fingers
And leave an angered, empty fist.

They wait, obsequious as darkness,
Quick to retire, quick to return;
Admit no aims or ethics; flatter
With reservations; will not learn

To answer to their names; are seldom
Truly owned till shot and skinned.
Cats, no less liquid than their shadows,
Offer no angles to the wind.

A. S. J. TESSIMOND

Zwei katzen *Franz Marc*

from: The Manciple's Tale
Mice before milk

Lat take a cat and fostre hym wel with milk
And tendre flessch and make his couche of silk,
And lat hym seen a mouse go by the wal,
Anon he weyvith milk and flessch and al,
And every deyntee that is in that hous,
Suich appetit he hath to ete a mous.

GEOFFREY CHAUCER

Cat and kittens *Francis Barlow*

The singing cat

It was a little captive cat
   Upon a crowded train
His mistress takes him from his box
   To ease his fretful pain.

She holds him tight upon her knee
   The graceful animal
And all the people look at him
   He is so beautiful.

But oh he pricks and oh he prods
   And turns upon her knee
Then lifteth up his innocent voice
   In plaintive melody.

He lifteth up his innocent voice
   He lifteth up, he singeth
And to each human countenance
   A smile of grace he bringeth.

He lifteth up his innocent paw
   Upon her breast he clingeth
And everybody cries, Behold
   The cat, the cat that singeth.

He lifteth up his innocent voice
   He lifteth up, he singeth
And all the people warm themselves
   In the love his beauty bringeth.

STEVIE SMITH

Choosing their names

Our old cat has kittens three—
What do you think their names should be?

One is tabby with emerald eyes,
   And a tail that's long and slender,
And into a temper she quickly flies
   If you ever by chance offend her.
      I think we shall call her this—
      I think we shall call her that—
Now, don't you think that Pepperpot
    Is a nice name for a cat?

One is black with a frill of white,
   And her feet are all white fur,
If you stroke her she carries her tail upright
   And quickly begins to purr.
      I think we shall call her this—
      I think we shall call her that—
Now, don't you think that Sootikin
    Is a nice name for a cat?

One is a tortoiseshell yellow and black,
   With plenty of white about him;
If you tease him, at once he sets up his back,
   He's a quarrelsome one, ne'er doubt him.
      I think we shall call him this—
      I think we shall call him that—
Now, don't you think that Scratchaway
    Is a nice name for a cat?

THOMAS HOOD

Studies of Cats from Miaulements *Théophile Steinlen*

To a cat

Stately, kindly, lordly friend
                    Condescend
Here to sit by me, and turn
Glorious eyes that smile and burn,
Golden eyes, love's lustrous meed,
On the golden page I read.

All your wondrous wealth of hair
                    Dark and fair,
Silken-shaggy, soft and bright
As the clouds and beams of night,
Pays my reverent hand's caress
Back with friendlier gentleness.

Dogs may fawn on all and some
                    As they come;
You, a friend of loftier mind,
Answer friends alone in kind.
Just your foot upon my hand
Softly bids it understand.

A. C. SWINBURNE

Girl and cat *Anonymous*

On the death of a cat
A friend of mine aged ten years and a half

Who shall tell the lady's grief
When her Cat was past relief?
Who shall number the hot tears
Shed o'er her, belov'd for years?
Who shall say the dark dismay
Which her dying caused that day?

Come, ye Muses, one and all,
Come obedient to my call;
Come and mourn with tuneful breath
Each one for a separate death;
And, while you in numbers sigh,
I will sing her elegy.

Of a noble race she came,
And Grimalkin was her name.
Young and old full many a mouse
Felt the prowess of her house;
Weak and strong full many a rat
Cowered beneath her crushing pat;
And the birds around the place
Shrank from her too close embrace.
But one night, reft of her strength,
She laid down and died at length:
Lay a kitten by her side
In whose life the mother died.
Spare her line and lineage,
Guard her kitten's tender age,
And that kitten's name as wide
Shall be known as hers that died.
And whoever passes by
The poor grave where Puss doth lie,
Softly, softly let him tread,
Nor disturb her narrow bed.

CHRISTINA ROSSETTI

Anathema of cats
from: Phylyp Sparowe

On all the whole nacyon
Of cattes wylde and tame;
God send them sorrow and shame!
That cat especyally
That slew so cruelly
My lytell pretty sparowe.

JOHN SKELTON

Court cat
from: Piers Plowman

Then ran ther a route of ratones, as it were,
And small mys with hem, mo than a thousand,
Comen til a conseil for here commune profit
For a cat of a court cam wher him likede
And overlap him lightliche and laghte him
        alle at wille,
And playde with some perilously, and putte him
        ther him likede.

WILLIAM LANGLAND

route of ratones : a crowd of rats
mys : mice
til a conseil : to take council
ther : where

Monsieur Pussy-Cat, blackmailer

C'est un grand Monsieur Pussy-Cat
Who lives on the mat
Devant un feu énorme
And that is why he is so fat,
En effet il sait quelque chose
Et fait chanter son hôte,
Raison de plus pourquoi
He has such a glossy coat.
Ah ha, Monsieur Pussy-Cat
Si grand et si gras,
Take care you don't *pousser trop*
The one who gives you such *jolis plats.*

STEVIE SMITH

Presbyterian cat
Hung for catching a mouse on the Sabbath

Then forth to exe-cu-ti-on,
Poor Baudrons she was drawn,
And on a tree they hanged her hie,
And then they sang a psalm.

ANONYMOUS

Churning *J.-F. Millet*

Cat

The black cat yawns,
Opens her jaws,
Stretches her legs,
And shows her claws.

Then she gets up
And stands on four
Long stiff legs
And yawns some more.

She shows her sharp teeth,
She stretches her lip,
Her slice of a tongue
Turns up at the tip.

Lifting herself
On her delicate toes,
She arches her back
As high as it goes.

She lets herself down
With particular care,
And pads away
With her tail in the air.

MARY BRITTON MILLER

*Detail of an illustration
to* Hudibras.
*From an engraving
by William Hogarth*

The retired cat

A poet's cat, sedate and grave
As poet well could wish to have,
Was much addicted to inquire
For nooks to which she might retire,
And where, secure as mouse in chink,
She might repose, or sit and think.
I know not where she caught the trick—
   Nature perhaps herself had cast her
In such a mould philosophique,
   Or else she learned it of her master.
Sometimes ascending, debonair,
An apple tree, or lofty pear,
Lodged with convenience in the fork,
She watched the gardener at his work;
Sometimes her ease and solace sought
In an old empty watering pot;
There, wanting nothing save a fan,
To seem some nymph in her sedan
Apparelled in exactest sort,
And ready to be borne to court.
   But love of change, it seems, has place,
Not only in our wiser race;
Cats also feel, as well as we,
That passion's force, and so did she.
Her climbing, she began to find
Exposed her too much to the wind,
And the old utensil of tin
Was cold and comfortless within:
She therefore wished instead of those
Some place of more serene repose,
Where neither cold might come, nor air
Too rudely wanton with her hair,
And sought it in the likeliest mode
Within her master's snug abode.

A drawer, it chanced, at bottom lined
With linen of the softest kind,
With such as merchants introduce
From India, for the ladies' use,
A drawer impending o'er the rest,
Half open in the topmost chest,
Of depth enough, and none to spare,
Invited her to slumber there;
Puss with delight beyond expression
Surveyed the scene, and took possession.
Recumbent at her ease, ere long,
And lulled by her own humdrum song,
She left the cares of life behind,
  And slept as she would sleep her last,
When in came, housewifely inclined,
The chambermaid, and shut it fast;
By no malignity impelled,
But all unconscious whom it held.
  Awakened by the shock (cried Puss)
'Was ever cat attended thus?
'The open drawer was left, I see,
'Merely to prove a nest for me,
'For soon as I was well composed,
'Then came the maid, and it was closed.
'How smooth these 'kerchiefs, and how sweet!
'Oh what a delicate retreat!
'I will resign myself to rest
'Till Sol, declining in the west,
'Shall call to supper, when, no doubt
'Susan will come and let me out.'
  The evening came, the sun descended,
And Puss remained still unattended.
The night rolled tardily away,
(With her indeed, 'twas never day),

The sprightly morn her course renewed,
The evening gray again ensued,
And puss came into mind no more
Than if entombed the day before.
With hunger pinched, and pinched for room,
She now presaged approaching doom
Nor slept a single wink or purred,
Conscious of jeopardy incurred.
   That night, by chance, the poet watching,
Heard an inexplicable scratching;
His noble heart went pit-a-pat,
And to himself he said—'What's that?'
He drew the curtain at his side,
And forth he peeped, but nothing spied.
Yet, by his ear directed, guessed
Something imprisoned in the chest,
And, doubtful what, with prudent care
Resolved it should continue there.
At length a voice which well he knew,
A long and melancholy mew,
 Saluting his poetic ears,
Consoled him and dispelled his fears:
He left his bed, he trod the floor,
He 'gan in haste the drawers to explore,
The lowest first, and without stop
The rest in order to the top.
For 'tis a truth well known to most
That whatsoever thing is lost,
We seek it, ere it come to light,
In every cranny but the right.
Forth skipped the cat, not now replete
As erst with airy self-conceit,
Nor in her own fond apprehension
A theme for all the world's attention

But modest, sober, cured of all
Her notions hyperbolical,
And wishing for a place of rest
Anything rather than a chest.
Then stepped the poet into bed,
With this reflection in his head.

Moral

Beware of too sublime a sense
Of your own worth and consequence:
The man who dreams himself so great,
And his importance of such weight,
That all around, in all that's done,
Must move and act for him alone,
Will learn in school of tribulation
The folly of his expectation.

WILLIAM COWPER

Dame Trot's cat *George Cruikshank*

The cat and the lute

Are these the strings that poets say
Have cleared the air, and calmed the sea?
Charmed wolves, and from the mountain crests
Made forests dance with all their beasts?
Could these neglected shreds you see
Inspire a lute of ivory
And make it speak? Oh! think then what
Hath been committed by my cat,
Who, in the silence of this night
Hath gnawed these cords, and ruined them quite,
Leaving such remnants as may be
'Frets'—not for my lute, but me.

Puss, I will curse thee; mayest thou dwell
With some dry hermit in a cell
Where rat ne'er peeped, where mouse ne'er fed,
And flies go supperless to bed.
Or may'st thou tumble from some tower,
And fail to land upon all fours,
Taking a fall that may untie
Eight of nine lives, and let them fly.

What, was there ne'er a rat nor mouse,
Nor larder open? nought in the house
But harmless lute-strings could suffice
Thy paunch, and draw thy glaring eyes?

Know then, thou wretch, that every string
Is a cat-gut, which men do spin
Into a singing thread: think on that,
Thou cannibal, thou monstrous cat!

Thou seest, puss, what evil might betide thee:
But I forbear to hurt or chide thee:

For maybe puss was melancholy
And so to make her blithe and jolly,
Finding these strings, she took a snatch
Of merry music: nay then, wretch,
Thus I revenge me, that as thou
Hast played on them, I've played on you.

THOMAS MASTER

Detail of Industry and Idleness Plate I. *William Hogarth*

Ode

On the death of a favourite cat
Drowned in a tub of gold fishes

'Twas on a lofty vase's side
  Where China's gayest art had dyed
  The azure flowers, that blow;
Demurest of the tabby kind,
The pensive Selima, reclined,
  Gazed on the lake below.

Her conscious tail her joy declared;
The fair round face, the snowy beard,
  The velvet of her paws,
Her coat, that with the tortoise vies,
Her ears of jet, and emerald eyes,
  She saw; and purr'd applause.

Still had she gazed; but 'midst the tide
Two angel forms were seen to glide,
  The genii of the stream:
Their scaly armour's Tyrian hue
Through richest purple to the view
  Betray'd a golden gleam.

The hapless nymph with wonder saw:
A whisker first, and then a claw,
  With many an ardent wish,
She stretch'd, in vain, to reach the prize
What female heart can gold despise?
  What cat's averse to fish?

Presumptuous maid! with looks intent
Again she stretch'd, again she bent,
  Nor knew the gulf between.
(Malignant Fate sat by, and smiled)
The slipp'ry verge her feet beguiled,
  She tumbled headlong in.

Eight times emerging from the flood
She mew'd to ev'ry wat'ry God,
   Some speedy aid to send.
No Dolphin came, no Nereid stirr'd:
Nor cruel Tom, nor Susan heard.
   A fav'rite has no friend!

From hence, ye beauties, undeceived,
Know, one false step is ne'er retrieved,
   And be with caution bold.
Not all that tempts your wand'ring eyes
And heedless hearts is lawful prize.
   Nor all that glitters, gold.

THOMAS GRAY

Cat eating a fish *from an ancient Egyptian painting*

Le chat

Viens, mon beau chat, sur mon cœur amoureux
   Retiens les griffes de ta patte,
Et laisse-moi plonger dans tes beaux yeux,
   Mêlés de métal et d'agate.

Lorsque mes doigts caressent à loisir
   Ta tête et ton dos élastique,
Et que ma main s'enivre du plaisir
   De palper ton corps électrique,

Je vois ma femme en esprit ; son regard,
   Comme le tien, aimable bête,
Profond et froid, coupe et fend comme un dard,

Et, des pieds jusques à la tête,
Un air subtil, un dangereux parfum,
   Nagent autour de son corps brun.

CHARLES BAUDELAIRE

Femme au chat *Auguste Renoir*

To a cat

Cat! who has pass'd thy grand climacteric,
   How many mice and rats hast in thy days
   Destroy'd?—How many tit bits stolen? Gaze
With those bright languid segments green, and prick
Those velvet ears—but pr'ythee do not stick
   Thy latent talons in me—and upraise
   Thy gentle mew—and tell me all thy frays
Of fish and mice, and rats and tender chick.
Nay, look not down, nor lick thy dainty wrists—
   For all the wheezy asthma,—and for all
Thy tail's tip is nick'd off—and though the fists
   Of many a maid have given thee many a maul,
Still is that fur as soft as when the lists
   In youth thou enter'dst on glass bottled wall.

JOHN KEATS

Rejoice in the Lamb
A song from Bedlam '

For I will consider my cat Jeoffry.

For he is the servant of the living God, duly and daily serving
him.

For at the first glance of the glory of God in the East he
worships in his way.

For this is done by wreathing his body seven times round
with elegant quickness.

For when he leaps up to catch the musk, which is the blessing
of God upon his prayer.

For he rolls upon prank to work it in.

For having done duty and received blessing he begins to
consider himself.

For this he performs in ten degrees.

For first he looks upon his fore-paws to see if they are clean.

For secondly he kicks up behind to clear away there.

For thirdly he works it upon stretch with the fore-paws
extended.

For fourthly he sharpens his paws by wood.

For fifthly he washes himself.

For sixthly he rolls upon wash.

For seventhly he fleas himself, that he may not be interrupted
upon the beat.

For eighthly he rubs himself against a post.

For ninthly he looks up for his instructions.

For tenthly he goes in quest of food.

For having consider'd God and himself he will consider his
neighbour.

For if he meets another cat he will kiss her in kindness.

For when he takes his prey he plays with it to give it [a]
chance.

For one mouse in seven escapes by his dallying.

For when his day's work is done his business more properly
begins.

For he keeps the Lord's watch in the night against the
    adversary.
For he counteracts the powers of darkness by his electrical
    skin and glaring eyes.
For he counteracts the Devil, who is death, by brisking about
    the life.
For in his morning orisons he loves the sun and the sun loves
    him.
For he is of the tribe of Tiger.
For the Cherub Cat is a term of the Angel Tiger.
For he has the subtlety and hissing of a serpent, which in
    goodness he suppresses.
For he will not do destruction, if he is well-fed, neither will
    he spit without provocation.
For he purrs in thankfulness, when God tells him he's a good
    Cat.
For he is an instrument for the children to learn benevolence
    upon.
For every house is incomplete without him & a blessing is
    lacking in the spirit.
For the Lord commanded Moses concerning the cats at the
    departure of the Children of Israel from Egypt.
For every family had one cat at least in the bag.
For the English cats are the best in Europe.
For he is the cleanest in the use of his fore-paws of any
    quadrupeds.
For the dexterity of his defence is an instance of the love of
    God to him exceedingly.
For he is the quickest to his mark of any creature.
For he is tenacious of his point.
For he is a mixture of gravity and waggery.
For he knows that God is his Saviour.
For there is nothing sweeter than his peace when at rest.
For there is nothing brisker than his life when in motion.

For he is of the Lord's poor and so indeed is he called by
    benevolence perpetually—Poor Jeoffry! poor Jeoffry! the rat
    has bit thy throat.

For I bless the name of the Lord Jesus that Jeoffry is better.

For the divine spirit comes about his body to sustain it in
    compleat cat.

For his tongue is exceeding pure so that it has in purity what
    it wants in musick.

For he is docile and can learn certain things.

For he can set up with gravity which is patience upon
    approbation.

For he can fetch and carry, which is patience in employment.

For he can jump over a stick which is patience upon proof
    positive.

For he can spraggle upon waggle at the word of command.

For he can jump from an eminence into his master's bosom.

For he can catch the cork and toss it again.

For he is hated by the hypocrite and miser.

For the former is afraid of detection.

For the latter refused the charge.

For he camels his back to bear the first motion of business.

For he is good to think on, if a man would express himself
    neatly.

For he made a great figure in Egypt for his signal services.

For he killed the Icneumon-rat very pernicious by land.

For his ears are so acute that they sting again.

For from this proceeds the passing quickness of his attention.

For by stroaking of him I have found out electricity.

For I perceived God's light about him both wax and fire.

For the Electrical fire is the spiritual substance, which God
    sends from heaven to sustain the bodies both of man and
    beast.

For God has blessed him in the variety of his movements.

For, tho he cannot fly, he is an excellent clamberer.

For his motions upon the face of the earth are more than
    other quadrupeds.
For he can tread to all the measures upon the musick.
For he can swim for life.
For he can creep.

CHRISTOPHER SMART

The domestic cat *Thomas Bewick*

A true cat
(Air: *Spirituosi*)

Cats I scorn, who sleek and fat,
Shiver at a Norway Rat;
Rough and hardy, bold and free,
Be the cat that's made for me!
He, whose nervous paws can take
My lady's lapdog by the neck;
With furious hiss attack the hen,
And snatch a chicken from the pen.
If the treacherous swain should prove
Rebellious to my tender love,
My scorn the vengeful paw shall dart,
Shall tear his fur, and pierce his heart.

Chorus

Qu-ow wow, quall, wawl, moon.

ANNA SEWARD

An appeal to cats in the business of love

Ye Cats that at midnight spit love at each other,
Who best feel the pangs of a passionate lover,
I appeal to your scratches and your tattered fur,
If the business of love be no more than to purr.
Old Lady Grimalkin with her gooseberry eyes,
Knew something when a kitten, for why she was wise;
You find by experience, the love-fit's soon o'er,
Puss! Puss! lasts not long, but turns to *Cat-whore*!

   Men ride many miles,
   Cats tread many tiles,
  Both hazard their necks in the fray;
   Only Cats, when they fall
   From a house or a wall,
  Keep their feet, mount their tails, and away!

THOMAS FLATMAN

70

Amorous cats *Masugawa Hanzan*

The return of Ulysses (Detail) *Pinturicchio*

Montaigne's cat
from: The Compleat Angler

'. . . as the learned and ingenious Montaigne says like himself freely, When my cat and I entertain each other with mutual apish tricks, as playing with a garter, who knows but that I make my cat more sport than she makes me? Shall I conclude her to be simple, that has her time to begin or refuse to play as freely as I myself have? Nay, who knows but that it is a defect of my not understanding her language (for doubtless cats talk and reason with one another) that we agree no better? And who knows but that she pities me for being no wiser than to play with her, and laughs and censures my folly for making sport for her, when we two play together?'

IZAAK WALTON

Tiger at play

Whence hast thou then, thou witless Puss,
The magic power to charm us thus?
Is it, that in thy glaring eye,
And rapid movements we descry,
While we at ease, secure from ill,
The chimney corner snugly fill,
A lion darting at his prey?
.A tiger at his ruthless play?

JOANNA BAILLIE

Cats and birds *from an ancient Roman mosaic*

Cat into lady

A Man possessed a Cat on which he doted.
So fine she was, so soft, so silky-coated—
Her very mew had quality!
He was as mad as mad could be.
    So one fine day, by dint of supplications,
And tears, and charms, and conjurations,
He worked upon the Powers above
To turn her woman; and the loon
Took her to wife that very afternoon.
Before, 'twas fondness crazed him: now 'twas love!
Never did peerless beauty fire
Her suitor with more wild desire
Than this unprecedented spouse
Th' eccentric partner of her vows.
They spend their hours in mutual coaxing,
He sees each day less trace of cat,
And lastly, hoaxed beyond all hoaxing,
Deems her sheer woman, through and through;
Till certain mice, who came to gnaw the mat,
Disturbed the couple at their bill-and-coo.
The wife leapt up—but missed her chance;
And soon, their fears allayed by her new guise,
The mice crept back: this time she was in stance.
And took 'em by surprise.
Thenceforth all means were unavailing
T' eradicate her little failing.

The bent we are born with rules us till we die.
It laughs at schooling: by a certain age
The vessel smacks, the stuff has ta'en its ply.
Man strives in vain to disengage
His will from this necessity.
Our nature, so confirmed by use,
Binds us in chains that none may loose:

The dead mouse (Detail) *L. L. Boilly*

Whips and scorpions, brands and burns,
Leave it as it was before:
If you drive it through the door,
By the window it returns.

LA FONTAINE
    translated by Edward Marsh

Hodge
from: Life of Johnson

I never shall forget the indulgence with which he treated
Hodge, his cat; for whom he himself used to go out and buy
oysters, lest the servants having that trouble should take a
dislike to the poor creature. I am, unluckily, one of those who
have an antipathy to a cat, so that I am uneasy when in the
room with one; and I own, I frequently suffered a good
deal from the presence of the same Hodge. I recollect him
one day scrambling up Dr. Johnson's breast, apparently with
much satisfaction, while my friend, smiling and half-
whistling, rubbed down his back, and pulled him by the
tail; and when I observed he was a fine cat, saying, 'Why, yes,
Sir, but I have had cats whom I liked better than this'; and
then, as if perceiving Hodge to be out of countenance,
adding, 'but he is a very fine cat, a very fine cat indeed.'

JAMES BOSWELL

Le chat *Pablo Picasso*

Cat's eyes

The clever Chinese say they read
The time in eyes of cats.
In yours I see Time's greed,
A green or yellow season that's
Not Spring or Autumn but I fear
The passionate cruelty of youth
And cruel passionless old age,
While your eye's narrowed crescent swears
There is no comfort in the truth,
Love lives alongside rage.
The timeless clockwork creature purrs
In the same rhythm as man's heartbeat,
But like my heart both false and true
The coldness of your eye has ice's heat.
No man can read the time in me or you.

FRANCIS SCARFE

from:
Matthias

Rover, with the good brown head,
Great Atossa, they are dead;
Dead, and neither prose nor rhyme
Tells the praises of their prime.
Thou didst know them old and grey,
Know them in their sad decay.
Thou hast seen Atossa sage
Sit for hours beside thy cage;
Thou wouldst chirp, thou foolish bird,
Flutter, chirp—she never stirr'd!
What were now these toys to her?
Down she sank amid her fur;
Eyed thee with a soul resign'd—
And thou deemedst cats were kind!
—Cruel, but composed and bland,
Dumb, inscrutable and grand,
So Tiberius might have sat
Had Tiberius been a cat.

MATTHEW ARNOLD

The Graham Family (Detail) *William Hogarth*

The tortoiseshell cat

The tortoiseshell cat
She sits on the mat
As gay as a sunflower she;
In orange and black you see her blink,
And her waistcoat's white, and her nose is pink,
And her eyes are green of the sea.
But all is vanity, all the way;
Twilight's coming, and close of day,
And every cat in the twilight's gray,
Every possible cat.

The tortoiseshell cat,
She is smooth and fat,
And we call her Josephine,
Because she weareth upon her back
This coat of colours, this raven black,
This red of the tangerine.
But all is vanity, all the way;
Twilight follows the brightest day,
And every cat in the twilight's grey,
Every possible cat.

PATRICK R. CHALMERS

From a woodcut by Thomas Bewick

To my cat
(Le Chat Noir)

Half loving-kindliness and half disdain,
Thou comest to my call serenely suave,
With humming speech and gracious gestures grave
In salutation courtly and urbane:
Yet must I humble me thy grace to gain
For wiles may win thee, but no arts enslave,
And nowhere gladly thou abidest, save
Where nought disturbs the concord of thy reign,
Sphinx of my quiet hearth
Thou deignst to dwell,
Friend of my toil, companion of my ease,
Thine is the lore of Ra and Rameses;
That men forget thou dost remember well,
Beholden still in blinking reveries,
With sombre sea-green gaze inscrutable.

GRAHAM R. TOMSON

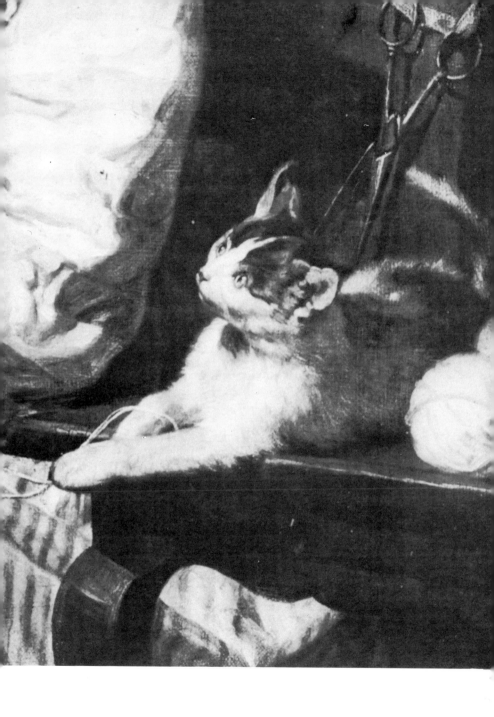

The wool winder (Detail) *J.-P. Greuze*
(Copyright The Frick Collection, New York)

The white cat of Trenarren
(for Beryl Cloke)

He was a mighty hunter in his youth
At Polmear all day on the mound, on the pounce
For anything moving, rabbit or bird or mouse—
My cat and I grow old together.

After a day's hunting he'd come into the house
Delicate ears stuck all with fleas.
At Trenarren I've heard him sigh with pleasure
After a summer's day in the long-grown leas—
My cat and I grow old together.

When I was a child I played all day,
With only a little cat for companion,
At solitary games of my own invention
Under the table or up in the green bay—
My cat and I grow old together.

When I was a boy I wandered the roads
Up to the downs by gaunt Carn Grey,
Wrapt in a dream at end of day,
All round me the moor, below me the bay—
My cat and I grow old together.

Now we are too often apart, yet
Turning out of Central Park into the Plaza,
Or walking Michigan Avenue against the lake-wind,
I see a little white shade in the shrubbery
Of far-off Trenarren, never far from my mind—
My cat and I grow old together.

When I come home from too much travelling,
Cautiously he comes out of his lair to my call,
Receives me at first with a shy reproach
At long absence to him incomprehensible—
   My cat and I grow old together.

Incapable of much or long resentment,
He scratches at my door to be let out
In early morning in the ash moonlight,
Or red dawn breaking through Mother Bond's spinney—
   My cat and I grow old together.

No more frisking as of old,
Or chasing his shadow over the lawn,
But a dignified old person, tickling
His nose against twig or flower in the border,
Until evening falls and bed-time's in order,
Unable to keep eyes open any longer
He waits for me to carry him upstairs
To nestle all night snug at foot of bed—
   My cat and I grow old together.

Careful of his licked and polished appearance,
Ears like shell-whorls pink and transparent,
White plume waving proudly over the paths,
Against a background of sea and blue hydrangeas—
   My cat and I grow old together.

A. L. ROWSE

A Cat
I keep, that plays about my
        House,
Grown fat
With eating many a miching
        Mouse.

ROBERT HERRICK

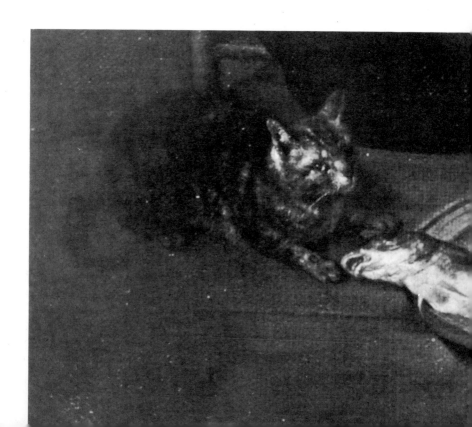

Love song
from: The Owl and the Pussy-Cat

'O lovely Pussy! O Pussy, my love,
  What a beautiful Pussy you are,
      You are,
      You are!
  What a beautiful Pussy you are!'

EDWARD LEAR

An old woman asleep (Detail) *Gabriel Metsu*
(Reproduced by permission of the Trustees of the Wallace Collection)

from:
Cats

Those who love cats which do not even purr,
Or which are thin and tired and very old,
Bend down to them in the street and stroke their fur
And rub their ears and smooth their breast, and hold
Their paws, and gaze into their eyes of gold.

FRANCIS SCARFE

Marigold

She moved through the garden in glory, because
She had very long claws at the end of her paws.
Her back was arched, her tail was high,
A green fire glared in her vivid eye;
And all the Toms, though never so bold,
Quailed at the martial Marigold.

RICHARD GARNETT

Studies of cats from Miaulements *Théophile Steinlen*

The cat and the rain

Careful observers may foretell the hour
(By sure prognostics) when to dread a shower;
While rain depends, the pensive cat gives o'er
Her frolics, and pursues her tail no more.

JONATHAN SWIFT

On a cat, ageing

He blinks upon the hearth rug,
And yawns in deep content,
Accepting all the comforts
That Providence has sent.

Loud he purrs and louder,
In one glad hymn of praise
For all the night's adventures,
For quiet restful days.

Life will go on for ever,
With all that cat can wish,
Warmth and the glad procession
Of fish and milk and fish.

Only – the thought disturbs him –
He's noticed once or twice
The times are somehow breeding
A nimbler breed of mice.

ALEXANDER GRAY

Studies of cats *Leonardo da Vinci*

Ode to a fat cat

Unhatch you April butterflies
For Maud is in a drawer.
Filling the air
With piles of overnourished fur.

Come crown the wonder of such startling size,
And tiny fish bones, spaced with violets, twine
To wreath the tips of those twin ears,
While down the graceful tabby-speckled spine
Lay bows in rows,
And round white paws
That out-vie Venus or the Himalayan snows.

Those strange and ornamental eyes
Stare with shifting sights,
Cavernous
Readily ravenous,
Lugubrious with subtle feline sighs.

And irresistible, the monster skittish pat
Of prima donna paw
Stretched from silky depths of flowing fur and fat,
Most exquisite!

And so I sing
To matchless Maud
Squatting in a drawer in Spring.

ANNABEL FARJEON

Wide-awake tortoiseshell cat *Gwen John*

The scribe's cat

I and Pangur Bán, my cat,
'Tis a like task we are at:
Hunting mice is his delight,
Hunting words I sit all night.

ANONYMOUS (eighth century)
Translated from the Irish by Robin Flower

Epitaph for Bathsheba

To whom none ever said scat,
No worthier cat
Ever sat on a mat
Or caught a rat:
Requies-cat

J. G. WHITTIER